Yesterday's Tampa

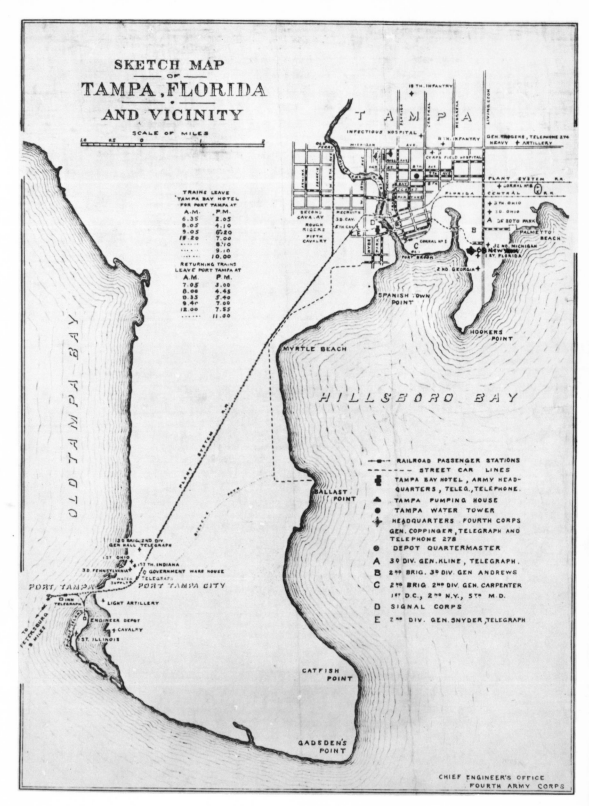

Sketch Map of Tampa and Vicinity, 1898

Yesterday's TAMPA

By Hampton Dunn

E. A. Seemann Publishing, Inc.
Miami, Florida

Second Printing, 1972
Third Printing, 1973
Fourth Printing, 1974
Fifth Printing, 1975

First paperback edition, 1977

Copyright © 1972 by George S. Neuman
Library of Congress Catalog Card Number: 72-82937
ISBN 0-912458-92-5

Manufactured in the United States of America

To my four favorite Florida "Crackers" –
my wife Charlotte and our three children, Janice, Hank, and Dennis–
all of them native Tampans; and to a sweet
little "Yankee" girl, Hank's wife Susie,
with affection.

Contents

Seemann's Historic Cities Series No. 1

Foreword

The seed for *Yesterday's Tampa* was planted one night last Spring during the Kiwanis travelogue series at McKay Auditorium when I learned from Henry Cox of Tampa Photo Supply Co., Inc., that he had acquired the entire collection of negatives of the Burgert Bros. commercial photographers. The Burgerts had recorded the pictorial history of Tampa for more than a half century. None were more professionally qualified or better photographers than this firm. But since the brothers had retired and passed away, their negatives were sold once or twice until Henry Cox learned of their availability. He bought them to assure their safekeeping. We worked out an arrangement for the publication rights, and this book is the first use I have made of them.

Not all communities have the advantage of being the subject of pictures taken over such a long period by such capable photographers as the Burgerts. It is my wish that the valuable collection will be perpetuated through publication in this and other volumes.

Tampa's is a thrilling story. I have tried to highlight our history in the narrative that accompanies the fine pictures. I have tried to reflect yesterday's Tampa in words and in photos, to share the legacy of this great city which I have learned to love over a period of some thirty-seven years.

Tampa, Florida   HAMPTON DUNN

Mud Flats to Metropolis

A Brief Sketch of Tampa's Colorful Background

Tantalizing Tampa Bay, as ideal and scenic and natural a port as could be found in the new world, has attracted visitors and permanent residents to the near tropical community on the Florida West Coast throughout history.

In fact, there have been inhabitants of this area back in the most ancient of recorded times. The Indians found this a desirable place to live, with its abundance of sea food, plentiful game in the forests, and rich soil suitable for producing fruits and vegetables. There are signs of these people around the Bay. Significant Indian mounds are accessible at Phillipi Park in what is now Pinellas County but for many years was part of Hillsborough, and at Terra Ceia Island in what is now Manatee, but originally also in Hillsborough County.

The area was settled by the Calusans and the Timucuans, each a hardy breed of red men. Friction developed between the Indians and the white men even before the Spanish conquistadores came to capture and to loot the land. The Spaniards living on nearby islands in the Caribbean had often raided those shores and taken away Indians to serve as their slaves. The tales of their mistreatment of the slaves spread rapidly among the tribes who remained in Florida. And that is why the first white "tourist" got such a "hot" reception.

Ponce de León was the first of a string of Spaniards to explore the wilds of Florida and to sail the waters of Tampa Bay. He came first in 1513, landed near St. Augustine on the East Coast, then wound his way around to Charlotte Harbor, near present-day Punta Gorda and Fort Myers, where he

TAMPA'S LATIN TIES go back to the very beginning of the settlement of the North American continent by the white man. The author reads the inscription on the monument in Plant Park commemorating the landing of Pánfilo de Narváez in Tampa Bay on Good Friday, April 15, 1528.

established a base until the Indians made it so uncomfortable for him that he decided to go back home and come again another day. It was not until eight years later, in 1521, that Ponce de León made it back to Florida. This time he sailed directly to Charlotte Harbor, and this time he planned to stay. He went up and down the West Coast, in all probability putting in in the big, safe harbor of Tampa Bay. But it was on this journey that the daring conquistador became the target of the local Indians. He was mortally wounded; his men got him back as far as Cuba where he died. Ponce de León's body rests in a tomb in the magnificent Cathedral of Saint John the Baptist in San Juan, Puerto Rico.

Someone has written that the Indians who fought the white invaders in Florida were "too tough to conquer and too stubborn to convert." The hostility was to remain many years and it was not until the Indian Wars of the 1830's that the red men were finally subdued.

More than a decade passed before the next important white visitor arrived in Tampa land. He was fiery, boisterous Pánfilo de Narváez, who had been with Cortez down in Mexico and had lost one eye in his exploits there. He and Cortez had a falling out, and Pánfilo rounded up an expedition to Tampa Bay. He landed on Good Friday of 1528. He was a persevering, ambitious explorer determined to find gold, silver, and all the other treasures the Spaniards expected to find in abundance in Florida. But Narváez' public relations were atrocious. The first thing he did after landing his party, probably in the vicinity of St. Petersburg, was to get into a hot argument with the Indian chief of the whole Tampa Bay region. Pánfilo drew his sword and sliced off a bit of the Chief's nose with its sharp blade. The Chief's mother interceded in behalf of her son, whereupon, the story goes, Narváez turned loose his dogs on the woman. Small wonder, then, that the word spread fast from tribe to tribe throughout the state about the invaders, and Narváez soon was persona non grata in the peninsula. His party made its way upstate as far as the St. Marks area south of the present-day capital of Tallahassee.

[12]

He had been scheduled to rendezvous with the boats he left in Tampa Bay that had been sent back to Cuba for supplies. By the time Narváez reached North Florida, the expedition's supplies and rations were exhausted and many men and horses had died en route. The boats never showed up, and the remaining party had to build some crude ships and put out to sea. A hurricane soon wiped out the little fleet. Only a few men survived. One was the official chronicler of the voyage, Cabeza de Vaca who was the first to put in writing that Tampa is "the best port in the world." Generations have come to agree with him.

Pánfilo de Narváez has long been gone—but he is not forgotten in Tampa. In 1928 an impressive marker was erected in Plant Park and it was identified as "commemorating the 400th anniversary of the landing of Pánfilo de Narváez, intrepid Spanish explorer, and his four hundred brave companions, the first white men to set foot upon the shores of Tampa Bay, April 15, 1528."

The writer of the inscription apparently assumed that Ponce de León did not reach these parts, a point of argument among scholars for centuries.

In 1539 there was another famous conquistador who called on Tampa, Hernando de Soto, who landed near Bradenton where a National Memorial marks his arrival. Legend has it that de Soto tramped through the woods to the site of the present-day teeming Tampa. For those who like legends, there is the one that de Soto met with the Indians under the giant "Charter Oak" in Plant Park in front of what is now the University of Tampa where he hammered out a treaty with them. De Soto kept moving, however, and roamed as far as the Mississippi River and beyond before his death at the riverside on his return journey.

It was in the Tampa Bay area that de Soto picked up young Juan Ortiz, said to be the only survivor of a small party the wife of Narváez sent to Florida to search for her missing husband. Young Juan was saved from torture and destruction by the Indians when a pretty Indian princess, daughter of the local chieftain, pleaded with her father to save the white lad's life. So, you see, Tampa had its own version of "Pocahontas" long before the John Smith affair up in Virginia nearly three quarters of a century later!

Other explorers came this way in later years; for instance, the founder of St. Augustine, Pedro Menéndez. This adventurer probed the West Coast as well as the east side of the state. But, actually, for a century after that, the Spanish virtually ignored the Gulf coast of Florida.

Time passed and eventually Tampa came to life with a few settlers other than Indians. A settlement developed in what is now the Hyde Park section

HERNANDO DE SOTO passed this way. Legend has it that the Spanish conquistador in 1539 nego-
tiated with the Indians underneath this giant oak that still provides shade in Plant Park on the
University of Tampa campus. This photo was taken in 1922.

of Tampa and known as Spanishtown on Spanishtown Creek (which
was covered over as a WPA project in the 1930's because so many children
had lost their lives in the stream). These were hardy pioneers, Spanish
and Cuban fishermen, who peacefully coexisted with the Indians. Not
long ago, a Tampa historian, Tony Pizzo, himself of Latin extraction, wrote
a book to explode the widespread belief that the Latin element came to
Tampa first in 1886 with the advent of the cigar industry and creation of
Ybor City. His delightful volume, "Tampa Town—Cracker Village With a
Latin Accent" documented the Latin flavor of this community through
the centuries.

Spain renewed its interest in the Florida West Coast in the 18th century.
And in April, 1757, an important visitor to the area was Don Francisco
Maria Celi, here on the vital mission of mapping Tampa Bay and the Hillsborough River. This document is "rich in information," according to Captain
John D. Ware, a present day harbor pilot in these waters and a historian
specializing in the background of Tampa Bay where he pilots seagoing ships
daily.

It was about this time, during the 1700's, that the pirates were active

[14]

along the Florida coastline and the Caribbean waters. Indeed, Tampa has an annual celebration dedicated to the proposition that one of the rascals will be remembered forever. It's the Gasparilla Carnival that recognizes the feats of a Spaniard, José Gaspar, who reputedly was the scourge of the Spanish Main until he finally met his match in the year 1821 as he was trapped by a U.S. Navy warship. José reportedly draped himself in the anchor chain of his own pirate ship and jumped overboard to his death, shouting his last words: "Gasparilla dies by his own hand, not the enemy's."

José Gaspar, fact or fiction, is remembered in another way in Tampa. In Welburn Guernsey's mobile home park, Guernsey City, at Gandy Boulevard and West Shore, there is a statue of a pirate, said to be the only statue to a rogue in the world. In any event, Tampa has a lot of fun every year saluting José, and many Tampans play pirates themselves on these festive occasions.

There was a period in the history of Florida that the state was under the rule of the British. This was from 1763—when the Spanish swapped Florida to England for Havana—until 1783, a few years after the American Revolution, during which Floridians remained loyal to the British Crown. And, it was during this period that the name Hillsborough enters the story. The river and the bay, as well as the county of which Tampa is county seat, by that name pays tribute to Lord Hillsborough, British Colonial Secretary of State in 1772.

Florida became a territory of the United States in 1821 when General Andrew Jackson, later president of the nation, took charge as our state's first governor. For several decades, the military was strong in running affairs of the primitive peninsula. And that's how the Tampa community really came into being.

The U.S. Army began erecting a network of army forts throughout the state to put down the Indian adversaries. And so it was in the Spring of 1824 that Fort Brooke was established on the site of present-day Tampa. It was named for and was under command of Colonel George Mercer Brooke. The farm and fishing village which grew up outside the military reservation also was called Fort Brooke but eventually was known by the Indian name of Tampa.

Colonel and Mrs. Brooke made history when they became parents of the first white child born in the area on December 18, 1826. "It's a boy!" they proudly announced and called him John. The lad grew up and became famous in his own right. He was graduated from the U.S. Naval Academy and, during the Civil War, served as Chief of Ordnance of the Confederate Navy and was in charge of converting the U.S.S. *Merrimac* into the world's first ironclad warship, the C.S.S. *Virginia.*

OLD CAREW HOMESTEAD at Franklin and Platt Streets in the year 1846. Dr. Edmund S. Carew was a pioneer Tampan who acquired a huge tract of land for homesteading.

The area got its first post office—but not much mail—in 1831 when the Tampa Bay Post Office, as it was called, opened. Schooners running along the coast brought the only word from the outside world.

In 1834, the County of Hillsborough was established by the Territorial Legislature when it was cut out of the old Alachua County. The new Hillsborough, Polk, Pinellas, Pasco, Manatee, Sarasota, Charlotte, DeSoto, Hardee and Highlands. Even so, the first census of the new county, taken in 1840, recorded only ninety-six civilians!

The violence of the Seminole War was brought home sadly to Tampa one cold day in December in 1835. A popular local Army officer, Major Francis L. Dade, was en route from Fort Brooke to Fort King, near Ocala, with a detachment of 100 soldiers scheduled to reinforce Army strength in the heart of the war front. The marching unit was ambushed and virtually wiped out that day at Bushnell, present day county seat of Sumter County. Major Dade was the first soldier to be struck and killed by the Indian bullets. Dade County, of which Miami is county seat, was created about this time and was named in honor of the fallen hero. The town of Dade City, county seat of Pasco County, also is named in recognition of the brave officer's deed.

Florida became a state in 1845 and Tampa became an incorporated town in 1855.

One of the greatest disasters ever to hit Tampa was the violent hurricane of September, 1848. The small community was lashed hard by high winds and high waters.

A little more than a decade later, more trouble brewed for Tampa. The

[16]

FORT BROOKE still was a quiet, isolated outpost for the U.S. military in 1880. The fort was activated in 1823 and named for the first commander, Brevet Colonel George Mercer Brooke. Colonel Brooke's son, John, was the first white child of Anglo-American parents born in the Tampa area, on December 18, 1826.

whole country was involved in a Civil War, and Tampans cast their lot with other Floridians on the side of the Confederacy. The community proudly sent a unit called "The Sunny South Guards" to the fighting front. At home, Federal Naval vessels sought to end blockade running in the busy Tampa port. There was some shelling of the city, but it was of no major consequence.

It took Tampa, Florida, and the South a long time to recover from the Civil War and the Reconstruction days that followed. There was an extended gloomy period during which the city just dragged along.

Then, suddenly, one day in 1885, Tampans decided to build a great city.

THE PORT OF TAMPA presented this busy sight to an artist who drew this pen and ink sketch in 1880. This is Tampa Bay from the mouth of the river.

Tampa, Fla., 1882   Population 400

"LITTLE FISHING VILLAGE" on Tampa Bay was the apt description of Tampa when this old picture was made in 1882. This is the view looking at Florida Avenue and Lafayette Street (Now John F. Kennedy Boulevard) from the old courthouse.

That was the day, May 7, when an enthusiastic Board of Trade was organized and a body of inspired citizens set about to transform Tampa from a tiny fishing village into a throbbing, productive metropolis.

They were no longer content to reside in a faded military outpost by the water, an isolated spot with deep, sandy streets, a few board sidewalks, only frame buildings and no industry or commerce to speak of.

The truth is the community at that moment stood at the threshold of development, but the rank and file of the citizenry were not fully aware of it.

Henry Bradley Plant just the year before had brought his railroad here from Sanford, providing a lifeline to the outside world. No longer would Tampa have to depend on a creaky stage coach from Gainesville, or on even slower boats from Key West or Cedar Key, or an ox-cart transportation over primitive trails, for communication. Also, a fabulous new industry was just beginning to grow: Phosphate pebbles had been discovered in the area.

Though the platform was set for action, the citizens until May 7 of that year had been hesitant to strike out boldly toward the future. Most of the local folk had lived through a long period of gloom, when it appeared Tampa was destined to dry up and blow away, ever since the closing of Fort Brooke,

[18]

the military installation that had been the sole reason for the town's existence in the first place. Indeed, in the period of the 1870's—the "Dismal
Decade," if you will—the village had lost population and had shrunk to
something like 726 souls when the 1880 census was taken. But with the
advent of Plant's railroad, growth came suddenly, almost a population explosion. By 1885, Tampa's population had increased to nearly 3,000 residents.

That's the way it was, on that fateful May 7, when they held a mass
meeting at the recently-opened Branch's Opera House for the purpose of
forming a Board of Trade, predecessor to today's Greater Tampa Chamber of
Commerce. The top people were on hand, and twenty-seven early birds were
"enrolled" as charter members that first meeting.

To lead these boosters in their crucial first year, those present chose Dr.
John P. Wall, a highly-respected physician who was not only a natural local
leader but an outstanding Floridian as well. Those pioneers moved swiftly,
and accomplished much. In its first year of operation, the Board of Trade
compiled a fantastic record. Take a look:

1. Lead a movement in support of City water works.
2. Advertised for and attracted ice factories here to serve a fast-growing
fish industry.
3. Spurred governmental action to erect a bridge across the Hillsborough
River, a community requirement Plant demanded before he would construct
the world's most beautiful accommodation, the Tampa Bay Hotel, in Hyde
Park on the west side of the stream. In addition, the civic leaders knocked
down opposition to the hotel project, which had been ridiculed by some and
fought by a few downtown merchants who wanted the hostelry built on the
east side of the river where the people were. Also, during the year, the Board
of Trade gave a gala reception and banquet to entertain Mr. and Mrs. Plant
lavishly and to let them know the town was grateful for their help in building Tampa.
4. Brought to Tampa its first major industry—cigar manufacture—with
the Board of Trade members personally underwriting the $4,000 needed to
seal the deal for land bought by V. Martinez Ybor to establish what became
Ybor City and a flourishing cigar town.
5. By proving that the cigar industry was coming and would bring sizable
payrolls here, the Board saved for the community its lone struggling bank
that was about to fold and move back to Jacksonville, the Bank of Tampa—
the predecessor to today's First National Bank.
6. Pushed for and got quick action from the U.S. Government in settling

claims upon land formerly occupied by Fort Brooke "so that the growth of the town will not be retarded."

7. Memorialized Congress for an appropriation to survey of the local ship's channel.

8. Raised funds for the relief of victims of the "recent conflagration" in Key West.

All these community accomplishments in one year, and Tampa at the crossroads had turned into the direction of greatness.

Practically from its beginning as a community, Tampa provided leadership at the state level, including the versatile Dr. Wall. The city sent its first citizen to the Governor's chair in 1892 when Henry Laurens Mitchell began a four-year term. Another Tampan to serve as Governor was Doyle E. Carlton (1929-1933).

Old-timers still repeat stories they heard from their forebears about "The Big Freeze" of 1894-95 which hit Tampa as well as much of the rest of the state. On December 29, 1894, the mercury dropped to 18 degrees in the city, and much lower than that in other parts of the state. And another cold spell came in February—bringing snowfall to Tampa for the first time in history! Citrus growers from North Florida began moving southward after that disastrous winter in hope of escaping the cold hazard in the future.

In the mid-Nineties, more trouble was brewing for the nation. A Cuban activist, José Martí, showed up in Tampa and made stirring speeches enlisting recruits to help overthrow the Spaniards in Cuba. They called Martí "the George Washington of Cuba." In 1898, the United States got involved, and the Spanish-American War was fought. Tampa became a focal point as some 30,000 troops were staged here for shipment to Cuba to wage war. The Tampa Bay Hotel became headquarters for the Army brass. A lesser-known officer, Teddy Roosevelt, arrived and was to gain fame in Cuba later as leader of his Rough Riders. After the conflict, he went on to become President of the United States.

After the turn of the century, action came on building a better port for Tampa. To Congressman Stephan M. Sparkman goes the credit for getting through Congress in 1905 an appropriation to finance the digging of the 20-foot port channel, which was the beginning of Tampa's great port development.

A setback to the city came on March 1, 1908, when a 20-block fire swept through Ybor City. It is believed to be the biggest area of Tampa ever burned. The fire damaged cigar factories and dwellings. It may have been started from an overheated kerosene stove, that was used in those days for

TAMPA'S FINEST HOTEL in 1883 was the handsome new H. B. Plant on Ashley Street near Lafayette Street. The owner, Jerry T. Anderson, named it in honor of the man who at the time was bringing the railroad to Tampa.

cooking. The city's firefighters were handicapped by lack of water because of small mains, some of them corroded.

An old brochure of the Tampa Board of Trade brags that "between 1890 and 1910, Tampa's growth was the greatest of any city of its class in the United States. The percent increase in population was 596. From 1900 to 1910 only one city in the Union made a greater gain in population than Tampa with its increase of 143.2 percent." The publication summed up the situation: "Since being a city the growth (of Tampa) has been nothing short of marvelous." It had only 720 residents in 1880, had 5,532 in 1890, and 15,838 in 1900. By 1910 there were 37,782.

Tampa made history on New Year's Day of 1914 when the world's first commercial airline service was inaugurated between St. Petersburg and

Tampa. Pilot of the pioneering aviation feat was Tony Jannus, who was killed in World War I.

The most shocking day in Tampa's history is said to be the day the stunned community received the week-old news of the wartime tragedy that had wiped out the lives of two dozen young Tampa sailors, along with fifteen other Floridians. It happened at nightfall on September 26, 1918, in the dark, cold waters of England's Bristol Channel. The city's own namesake, the U.S.S. *Tampa* had been sunk by a German torpedo. It is believed that this was the greatest single loss sustained by any community in the United States during World War I.

During World War I, Tampa became a shipbuilding center, and this activity was repeated in World War II two decades later.

For a considerable time in postwar Tampa, from 1920 to 1927, the community operated under the city-manager form of government. Charles H. Brown, prominent business man, was the first Mayor-Commissioner. The commission hired two city managers during its existence.

Another mighty hurricane struck the Tampa Bay area with devastating power in the early morning of October 25, 1921. It left in its wake at least two million dollars' damage in Tampa, and some five million dollars worth elsewhere in southern Florida. It was regarded as Tampa's worst blow since the big hurricane of 1848.

In the exciting days of the 1920's, Florida and Tampa underwent many significant changes. Tampa was linked directly to the Gulf beaches by the construction of Gandy Bridge to St. Petersburg (and a decade later, by the construction of Davis Causeway, now Courtney Campbell Parkway, to Clearwater). The foresighted builders who left these legacies were George S. (Dad) Gandy and Captain Ben T. Davis. Originally toll facilities, they were freed of tolls in 1944 when the Federal Government bought them and tore down the pay gates.

The dizzying Florida real estate boom was very much a part of Tampa's history in the Roaring Twenties; a daring developer, D. P. Davis, dredged up the bay and expanded a couple of mud flats islands, turning them into the city's most attractive residential section, only a few minutes' drive from downtown Tampa. The incredible Developer Davis sold $18 million dollars worth of lots even before the dredging was completed. In October, 1926, Davis sailed for Europe aboard the "Majestic," and was lost at sea. Some say he was swept overboard accidentally, while others suspect he threw himself overboard. An insurance company paid off on the $300,000 life insurance policy Davis took out just before he sailed.

[22]

As with all cities, Tampa has had many gruesome crimes in its records. But probably the most sensational, the one that stirred up the community the most, occurred in 1927 when a man identified as Benjamin Levins was arrested and charged with the brutal ax murders of Merman Merrill, his wife, and their four children. Levins was locked in the old County Jail on Pierce Street. Angry crowds began gathering at the jail and finally turned into a howling mob intent on storming the jail to get to the killer. The situation got so bad the Governor called out the National Guard to quell the rioters. Three persons were killed and nineteen others injured before the mob was brought under control.

The whole nation was thrown into chaos before the decade of the Twenties bowed out. The *Tampa Morning Tribune* shouted the news by way of an eight-column, 120 point streamer on October 25, 1929:

"BOTTOM DROPS OUT OF STOCKS"

The lead story from New York began: "The wild era of public speculation in stocks which has swept over the country during the past five years came to a climax today in the most terrifying stampede of selling ever experienced on the New York Stock Exchange. . . . "

But Tampa already was in the throes of a depression even before the rest of the country felt the shock waves. The Florida real estate boom had long since collapsed, leaving a lot of ghost towns, unfinished subdivisions, and paper fortunes almost worthless.

And then came what local historian Karl H. Grismer described as "a black day in the history of Tampa." That was July 17, 1929, the day the Citizen's Bank & Trust Co., one of the city's largest banking institutions, failed to open its doors for business, along with five smaller affiliated banks. Many depositors lost their entire savings, for an aggregate total of some $10 million, on that most lamentable and memorable "black day."

It ushered in the decade of the Great Depression, sometimes called "The Desperate Years." Some of Tampa's most affluent families found themselves jobless and on welfare. Soup lines formed as unemployment enveloped this large city of factories and plants. The Works Progress Administration (WPA), part of President Franklin D. Roosevelt's alphabet soup in the Federal Government made work for the unemployed. Tampa got some much-needed civic improvements out of it, including Peter O. Knight Airport, the widening of Bayshore Boulevard, a new seawall, repairs to the Tampa Bay Hotel, a new National Guard Armory, and many other WPA projects that kept people busy during the layoff period. There even were projects for writers and show people as well as for the unskilled.

[23]

Early in the decade of the Thirties, Tampa voters had approved a $750,000 bond issue to build an airport at Ballast Point. Pan American Airways had agreed to make Tampa the home base of its operations if a seaplane airport was provided. Selection of a site soon got bogged down in local politics—and Pan American moved its operations to Miami. The rest of that story is history—for Miami, not Tampa. Finally, however, Peter O. Knight Airport on Davis Islands was built and two airlines, National and Eastern, brought air service here.

It's an ill wind that brings no good, they say, so perhaps the Depression did bring some good to Tampa. For instance, the need became apparent for an institution of higher learning in our city to provide education at reasonable costs for local young men and women whose families could not afford to send them off to college. Into this void stepped a group of civic leaders who organized a community college, the University of Tampa. It began as a junior college in the Hillsborough High School facility in 1931, but by the Fall of 1933, it had become a full-fledged four-year university and moved into the long vacant Tampa Bay Hotel which provided ample space. The students were able to commute to college by streetcar from any part of the city at only five cents a trip. Today, University of Tampa alumni shine throughout Florida and the nation as teachers, lawyers, doctors, and business leaders. The university is still growing and expanding with the addition of numerous buildings.

Unrest surfaced from time to time during the depression years. Creeping communism became a concern of many of our people, and the Ku Klux Klan was evident. In 1935, the community was shocked by a brazen, terrifying flogging of several Tampans, some of whom died as the result. A young prosecutor, J. Rex Farrior, vigorously brought the alleged culprits to trial and halted this sort of vigilante activity.

Tampa's political structure reached its depth of corruptness early in the 1930's, and before the decade ended, a real reform was underway. In 1934, a rising young politician, Claude Pepper, was defeated in his initial bid for the U.S. Senate, because, as was generally conceded at the time, the election was stolen right here in Tampa. Those were the days of ballot box stuffing and election frauds. But a couple of years later, Pepper was elected and served in Congress, often as the eloquent spokesman for President Roosevelt. Pepper was defeated as Senator in 1950, but served in the U.S. House of Representatives as a Congressman from Miami for many years.

"Tampa's Longest Day" was September 3, 1935. The whole Labor Day weekend was turbulent, climaxed by election day on that Tuesday. They were without doubt the stormiest 24 hours in the history of the city. A violent hurricane struck Tampa at the same time city and county political forces were locked in a deadly confrontation that made our town an armed camp with police and sheriff's deputies and National Guardsmen colliding head-on. It was a day of "hot votes, fraudulent registrations, corrupt election officials, stolen ballot boxes, ballot box stuffing, dead men voting, cannon manned by guardsmen, a reckless display of machine guns, sawed-off shotguns, and a whole arsenal of weapons by an army of special city police and special sheriff's deputies."

The stage was set for reform. The *Tampa Morning Tribune* set the tone, along with the old *Tampa Daily Times,* in calling for a cleanup. The *Tribune* editorialized: "Let this be the last election with troops called out. How long is Tampa to admit it is at the mercy of job-seeking politicians and professional gamblers?" The *Times* said that the Sheriff's action in asking for the National Guard to keep order was a confession "which ought to make the heads of all self-respecting Tampans hang in shame. The situation is nothing less than sickening. Isn't it time that the people of Tampa who have no interest in factions and factionalism do something about it?"

The election scandals were such that civic-minded Tampans did, indeed, start a movement that resulted in bringing voting machines here and also provided top leaders for service on the Election Board and other reforms that did much to clean up the dirty mess. The iniquitous poll tax, long an evil in the state, was outlawed by the 1937 Legislature.

A recital of happenings in Tampa during the 1930's would be incomplete unless it mentions the sordid story of the gambling-political machine headed by Charlie Wall, the black sheep of a Tampa first family, who years later was blasted to death in a gangland killing. This is one of the bloody record of unsolved gangland murders that blackened the pages of the community's history then, and which are, to this very day, still unofficially "unsolved."

As this awesome decade came to a close, Tampa began gearing up for its role in World War II, just around the corner. The sprawling MacDill Air Force Base was started in 1939, with the first crews reporting in 1940. These were the first of tens of thousands of Air Force personnel who came through the gigantic air base during the following years. And MacDill continues, even in the 1970's, to be a vital cog in the nation's military machine.

Also, at the end of the Thirties, Tampa again became a tremendous shipbuilding center, turning out war ships and merchant vessels needed to help America win the worldwide conflict.

After V-J Day in 1945, the boys came home and Tampa entered into a period of postwar development. It scrapped its streetcars in 1946, and put in city buses. In 1953, a vast area of suburbs was annexed, ballooning the city's population to more than a quarter million persons. In 1958, the fabulous new University of South Florida was started. Shopping centers sprung up around the city, while the downtown area also underwent a face-lift, tearing out the railroad yards alongside Hillsborough River and replacing old structures with new skyscrapers. Urban renewal played a role in some of the cleanup.

A new Courthouse, new Police Station, new State Building and other public structures went up. With the advent of the national Interstate Highway System, expressways were brought to Tampa, where Interstate 75 and Interstate 4 helped solve the increasing traffic problem. And in 1971, the community proudly dedicated its ultra-modern international airport which is truly one of the world's finest air facilities.

In 1972 Tampa awaits another moment in history as it rushes toward completion the 35-story First National Bank Building in the heart of downtown, which, for a while at least, will be Florida's tallest structure.

Tampa has come a long way, indeed, since the days of the Caloosas and the Timucuans, the days of the Spanish conquistadores, the days of the desolate Fort Brooke, the pioneer days of the cigar industry, the boomtime period, the bustle of two world wars, the depressing days of the great depression, the days of postwar development, a long way to 1972, and the future looks bright.

Right: Plan of Tampa by John Jackson who in 1847 surveyed and drew the present plat of Tampa

PLAN
OF
TAMPA
1886

By John Jackson L.S.

Drawn in January

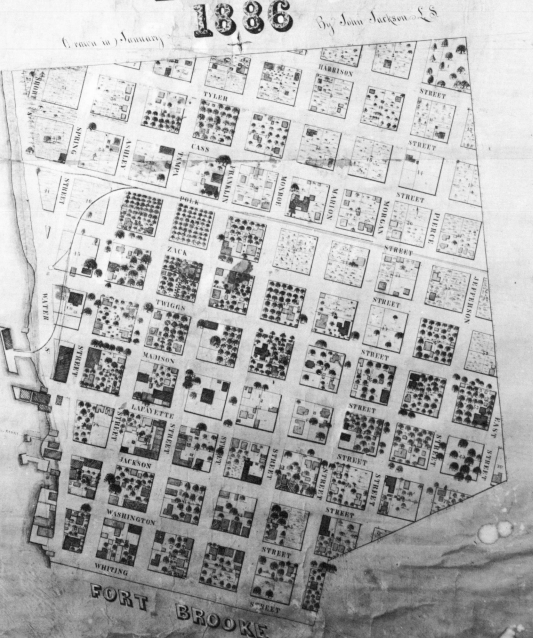

Tampa before 1900

THIS SHACK on Washington Street west of Franklin Street provided quarters for Tampa's first bank in 1883. T. C. Taliaferro, a forefather of present First National Bank president, E. P. Taliaferro, was then cashier of First National. It is believed the legend 'First National Bank' was drawn on the negative later, because at the time it was called 'Bank of Tampa'.

THE BEAUTIFUL PALMETTO HOTEL welcomed guests in 1884. The large frame structure dominated the skyline at Florida Avenue and Polk Street.

Previous page: BUSTLING FLORIDA AVENUE in 1884, looking south from the old Palmetto Hotel; the impressive building at center rear (with clock tower) is the first Hillsborough County Courthouse.

[30]

HILLSBOROUGH COUNTY'S FIRST COURTHOUSE at Florida Avenue and Madison Street, closed in by a picket fence, was built in 1855 and looked like this in 1886. The big mansion at far right belonged to pioneer Tampan, Captain James McKay.

DOWNTOWN VIEW IN 1884, looking northeast from the old county courthouse. Rambling wooden structure in center of photo was the old Academy of Holy Names.

TIBBETT'S CORNER, the southwest corner at Franklin Street and Lafayette Street (now John F. Kennedy Boulevard). Workmen are putting up the Tibbett's sign on top of the real estate building. The original business was a confectionary store run by the Tibbet brothers.

FIRST BRICK BUILDING in Tampa—and it's still standing—was the Bank of Tampa, predecessor of the First National Bank. Completed in February, 1886, at the southwest corner of Franklin and Washington Streets, it is now part of the Merchants Association of Tampa office building. Upon receiving a national charter on May 6, 1886, the bank adopted the new name, First National Bank.

DOUBLE-DECKER STREETCAR with a canopy on top hauled young people in the 1880's to the Ballast Point Pavilion for dances.

BY 1888, TAMPA NEEDED fire protection which was provided by the poorly equipped and under-manned Fire Department.

EXACT DATE OF THIS PORTRAIT of "Tampa's Finest," the Police Department, is not known; but it probably was posed in the late 1880's.

A TYPICAL TAMPA HOME and family in 1890 was that of City Marshal W. H. T. Ball on the west side of Marion between Twiggs and Marion. Picket fence kept out cows, pigs, and other animals in what is now busy downtown Tampa.

[34]

HEART OF THE CITY in 1890 was this busy corner at Franklin Street and Lafayette Street (now John F. Kennedy Boulevard). That's the Knight & Wall Building with the gazebo-like steeple. Streetcars provided "rapid transit" for Tampans of the day.

HERE'S FRANKLIN STREET looking north from Washington Street in 1890. The *Tampa Tribune* plant is at left. The elegant Almeria Hotel is at right, first "skyscraper" in the budding city. It still stands today, until recently serving as headquarters for the far-flung business empire of Lykes Bros.

THE TAMPA BAY HOTEL became a distinctive landmark when Henry B. Plant opened the fashionable hostelry in 1891. This photo, taken about that time, shows the new Lafayette Street bridge which city fathers agreed to construct as part of the lure to get Plant's fabulous structure. The city west of the river was pretty much wilderness at the time. The thirteen unique minarets atop the Spanish-Moorish-Turkish architecture represent the months in the Moslem calendar.

GARDENS AT TAMPA BAY—Henry B. Plant carried on a massive landscaping project to provide the proper setting for his exclusive resort hotel. The gardens in front of the hotel are now known as "Plant Park." They are named in honor of the railroad magnate who opened Tampa to development.

THE TAMPA BAY HOTEL reception room. Furnishings for the grand hotel were purchased by Mrs. Plant on a worldwide spending spree.

PARLOR, TAMPA BAY HOTEL. Exquisite furniture and decorations added to the warmth of the magnificent Tampa Bay Hotel.

UNIVERSITY OF TAMPA LOBBY. A latter-day photo of the Tampa Bay Hotel reception room. It still looks a great deal like this, as it now serves as the lobby for the main building of the University of Tampa. The sprawling structure now is called Plant Hall.

GLITTERING DINING ROOM of the Tampa Bay Hotel was the scene of numerous formal dinners. The old Florida Press Breakfasts began here. The Rotary Club and other groups used this facility in the early days. This room which served as the library for the University of Tampa for a number of years has been refurnished now as a dining room for special occasions.

EXCHANGE NATIONAL BANK opened on April 16, 1894, in the old quarters of the Gulf National Bank at the northeast corner of Franklin and Twiggs Streets. Posing in the door are bank employees C. J. Huber, R. M. Prince, Miss Elizabeth Asken, and Colonel T. B. Anderson. The latter was father of the prominent Tampans, J. B. and Otto Anderson. Note sign on second floor window identifying office of Peter O. Knight, for many years an outstanding attorney and leading citizen of Tampa.

YBOR CITY came into being in the mid-1880's when V. Martínez Ybor and other pioneer cigar manufacturers moved their factories here from Key West. Photo shows one of the first factories in Ybor City, as well as an early day dwelling.

YBOR CITY in 1898. The interurban trolley to Tampa moves through the suburb which grew up fast with the coming of the cigar industry. In 1898 the entire area of Tampa was bustling with activity because of the presence of troops debarking here for Cuba to fight the Spanish-American War.

WHEN THE CIGAR INDUSTRY was at its height, more than 13,000 cigar makers were employed to roll the stogies by hand. This view shows one floor of one of the large factories which lacked air-conditioning but seemed to have good cross ventilation from the numerous windows. Note the gentleman in high chair at right, the "reader" who entertained and informed the workers by reading out loud from daily newspapers and magazines.

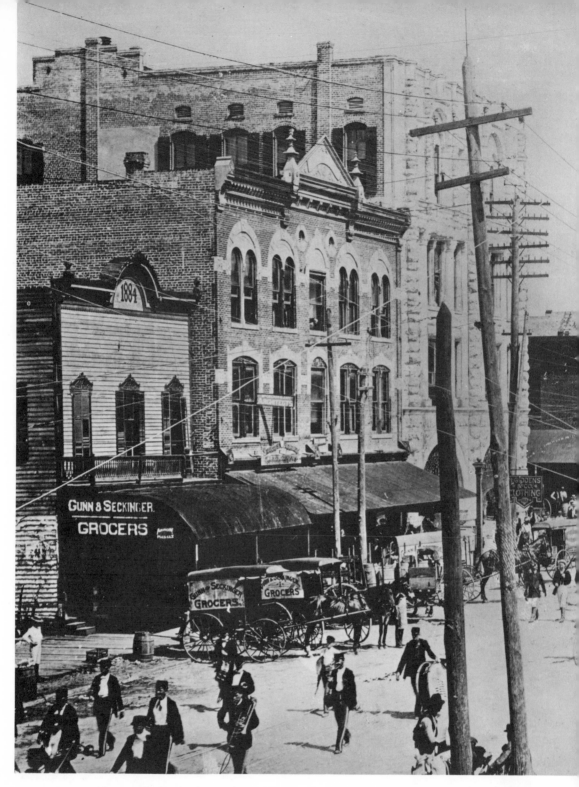

SPANISH AMERICAN WAR sparked a parade on Franklin Street in 1898. The tallest building on left

is the just completed First National Bank. The grocery offering speedy delivery was Gunn & Seckinger.

[42]

A CALVARY UNIT camps at Tampa during Spanish-American War. The mules were used to pull the cannon.

ARMY BRASS gathered in Tampa in 1898 when General Nelson Miles (wearing pith helmet) and his staff visited General Joe Wheeler (center front with white beard) and his staff during training for the Spanish-American War.

Left: ONE ARMY UNIT during the Spanish-American War camped in Tampa Heights. This was a typical scene in these hot, monotonous, dreary camps where some 30,000 troops were billeted.

THEODORE ROOSEVELT, later President of the United States, won fame in the Spanish-American War as the fearless leader of the Rough Riders.

ARMY CAMP LIFE was quiet at camps in the Tampa area as units prepared to go across the waters to fight in Cuba. Shown are officers quarters of the first Illinois at Picnic Island in 1898.

OFFICER'S QUARTERS - 1ST ILLINOIS, PICNIC ISLAND TAMPA, FLA. 1898

EL PASAJE RESTAURANT and hotel at Ninth Avenue and 14th Street in Ybor City was a popular place from the 1890s until the late 1930s. The brick structure still stands, although it's vacant. The elite stayed here during the old days. José Martí–"The George Washington of Cuba"–slept here as he plotted war against Spain. Army brass and war correspondents hung out here during training for the Spanish-American War. Florida governors, senators, and other political leaders were lavishly entertained here for decades.

COOLING SULPHUR SPRINGS was a popular recreational site in 1899, as it continues to be to this day. This is how is appeared way back then.

THIS ELEGANT LADY has been identified as Mrs. E. A. Clarke, prominent
citizen in the early 1900s.

[46]

OLD FIRST PRESBYTERIAN CHURCH at the southeast corner of Marion and Zack Streets at the
turn of the century.

Tampa from 1900 to 1919

LET'S GO CANOEING. A recreation-seeking couple boards a canoe at Temple Terrace for a cruise on the Hillsborough River, about 1900.

Previous page: A GOOD OVERVIEW OF TAMPA in 1906. This is a scene looking north from the Tampa Electric Company power plant stack on the Hillsborough River. The bridge in foreground is the Lafayette Street (now John F. Kennedy Boulevard) bridge. The old Tampa Bay Hotel (now University of Tampa) dominates the skyline at top left.

OLD YBOR CIGAR FACTORY at Ninth Avenue and 14th Street in Ybor City, about the turn of the century. It was on these steps that José Martí gave stirring speeches to enlist Tampans in the fight for Cuba's freedom in the mid-1890s.

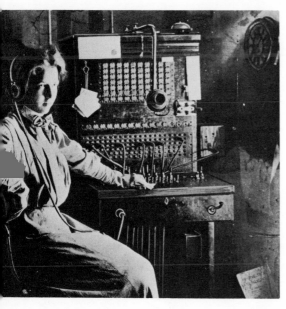

PRETTY SWITCHBOARD OPERATOR for Peninsula Telephone Company, predecessor of General Telephone Company, in 1902. Her name was Elsie Hart.

FIRST HEADQUARTERS FOR Peninsular Telephone Company in Tampa were in the old Roberts Building. In 1902, the business office was on the first floor, the operators on the second. The company founder, W. G. Brorein, is standing in the doorway.

CONSTRUCTION GANG of Peninsular Telephone Company (predecessor of General Telephone Company) pauses before its horse-drawn transportation in 1910.

HOW A BUSINESS OFFICE looked in the early 1900's when this picture of the Peninsular Telephone Company was taken.

THE UNITED STATES POST OFFICE and Courthouse was under construction on February 1, 1903. The old First Presbyterian Church at Marion and Zack Streets is seen in background. The three-story building on right has sign on front with the legend "DeSoto Hotel." At far left in background is a warehouse for Peninsular Telephone Company.

FLORIDA's FIRST CROSS-COUNTRY auto race was run in 1909 from Tampa to Jacksonville. The idea of *Tampa Times'* city editor Willis Powell, the event was co-sponsored by the *Times* and the Tampa Automobile Club. Eighteen cars took part in the rugged endurance feat which helped to spotlight the need for better roads in the state. The "pathfinding car" is shown as it arrived at the office of the *Jacksonville Metropolis* (precedessor to the *Jacksonville Journal*). In the car are B. Marion Reed, driver; L. R. Reagin, right front; T. N. Henderson, right rear, and Captain C. S. Washington. It took four days to make the round trip, averaging ten miles an hour. First prize went to Horace Williams of St. Petersburg.

THE SECOND BRIDGE across Hillsborough River at Lafayette Street in 1911 with the skyline of downtown Tampa in the background. The Atlantic Coast Line Railroad freight station and switchyard remained here until the late 1950's. *Right:* The opposite view, from Water Street looking west. There was a bargain at the French Dry Cleaners that day: "4 Suits cleaned for $1." *Below:* The bridge, looking east and south. Note the interesting gas lamps on the left and the mass of telephone wires overhead on the right.

BUSY DOWNTOWN TAMPA in 1911, looking north on Franklin Street from Lafayette Street. The streetcar shown served the Michigan Avenue (now Columbus Drive) run. The Courthouse Square is on the right. The new First National Bank Building boasted a marble front.

[54]

"FOR A BRIGHTER TAMPA" was the Tampa Electric Company's message on the street banner across Franklin Street in 1911. Maas the Haberdasher's store was on the left corner; across the street the doomed building housing the first home of the Citizen's Bank & Trust Company. Signs announced the law offices of Gunby & Gibbons and of William Hunter.

THIS IS HYDE PARK AVENUE in 1911, a lovely residential area with no traffic problems.

NEBRASKA AVENUE was a popular and atrractive residential street in 1911.

SOCIAL AND RECREATIONAL CENTER for Tampa in 1911 was the ornate and spacious Ballast

Point Pavilion seen here from the water.

OLD MALLORY DOCKS in 1911 at the Hendry & Knight Channel in Tampa's harbor which had just been deepened. Traffic increased, and the port became extremely congested. The Mallory Steamship Line ran steamers and schooners to New York, Key West, and Mobile.

A GOOD VIEW of South Franklin Street, looking south, in 1913. First building on left is at Washington Street and was the Almeria Hotel, in later years the headquarters for Lykes Bros. Across the street on the southeast corner of the intersection is the old Hotel Olive which later was added to and became Thomas Jefferson Hotel, which was torn down in the late 1960's. In the same block, next to the hotel, is the Buick agency, probably the Joe B. (for "Buick") Johnson firm at the time, later to become Giles Motor Co., headed by L. B. Giles, who sold it to Faircloth Buick Co. in the 1960's when it was moved to Dale Mabry Highway. The Seaboard Air Line station is the small brick building with awnings. On the southwest corner of Franklin and Washington is the home of the old *Tampa Daily Times* which expanded it and continued to use the structure until the sale of the newspaper on June 1, 1958, to the *Tampa Tribune*. The building still stands and is now occupied by the Merchants Association of Tampa. The Mallory docks are at the end of Franklin Street. In the distance at far right of photo are the tiny islands that were to be the basis of Davis Islands during the Florida real estate "boom" of the 1920's.

THE STURDY YMCA building on Florida Avenue as it looked in 1911. This institution has served generations of Tampans through the years. Originally built in 1908, the words on the cornerstone say "Christ Jesus Himself Being the Chief Cornerstone." The great orator and politician, William Jennings Bryan, spoke at the dedication. The building was badly damaged by fire in the early 1970's.

[59]

AS LATE AS 1912 the fountain for horses on the Courthouse Square was necessary, as this photograph of the Madison Street side shows. The shop across the street advertised Dodge Brothers Motor Cars, while the Hotel Royal next door awaits guests.

[60]

HYDE PARK was one of the most fashionable residential areas of the city in 1913. This is Hyde Park Avenue, looking south from the Tampa Bay Hotel. Hyde Park was subdivided in 1886 by O. H. Platt who named the section for his hometown in Illinois. The real estate development really "got off the ground" a few years later when Henry B. Plant built the magnificent Tampa Bay Hotel on the west side of the river.

GORRIE SCHOOL on South Boulevard in Hyde Park. Originally called the "Hyde Park School" (as in this 1913 photograph), it was later renamed in honor of Dr. John Gorrie of Apalachicola, who patented the first ice-making machine.

ALMOST AN AERIAL VIEW of Hyde Park is this picture taken in 1913 from the old Mugge Building and looking southwest from the Bay View Hotel. The Favorite Line steamship dock is in the foreground. The Tampa Electric Company power plant had only one smokestack at the time.

COURTHOUSE SQUARE in 1913, looking northeast from the Bay View Hotel. The Courthouse was built in 1891-92 at a cost of $60,000 by J. A. Wood, who designed the Tampa Bay Hotel, and torn down in 1952 after the new Courthouse had been erected.

THE FIRST AEROPLANE to be seen in Tampa is shown in flight in this history-making photograph taken in 1913.

THE FIRST COMMERCIAL PLANE in the world is shown in this old photograph. Tony Jannus made two round trips daily for 187 days. At right is photo of the first check made out to the Benoist Air Boat Company for $400 to pay first passage for A. C. Pheil.

[62]

COMMERCIAL AVIATION began on January 1, 1914 when the first commercial flight was made between St. Petersburg and Tampa. This photo is believed to be that of the pilot Tony Jannus in a plane of that vintage, even if not a passenger plane. The airline lasted for only a few weeks.

THE TAMPA GAS COMPANY was organized in 1895 but its product was not popular for home use for a number of years. The City of Tampa did install gas street lamps in 1898. *Above:* The headquarters building on the southeast corner of Tampa and Madison Streets in 1914 which also contained the Madison Hotel. *Below:* The 600,000 cubic foot storage tank was erected in 1912 as cooking with gas became popular.

A NOTABLE EVENT OF 1915 was the opening of Woodrow Wilson Junior High School on Swann Avenue. This school with its twin, George Washington Junior High School on Michigan Avenue (now Columbus Drive) enabled Tampa to take the lead in the reorganization of the school system. It changed from the traditional eight-year elementary and grammar school and four-year high school to the six-year elementary school, three-year junior high school, and three-year senior high school for the divisions of the standard 12-year course for the public schools of the city. Wilson Junior High continues to operate in this building to this day.

OLD CHILDREN'S HOME and its occupants in 1916. It was located in a large house at the corner of Washington and Marion Streets, donated by Mrs. C. A. Clark.

"TYPICAL FLORIDA HOME" is the descriptive caption of this photo from the Burgert Bros. collection. Large shade trees add to the serenity of the homesite. The home featured a porte-cochere and large verandas. This was probably "Greylocks" at 218 Lake Hollingsworth Drive in Lakeland. The original house was built in the mid-1800s by Spencer Minor Stephens, a pioneer Florida citrus grower. About 1928 it was acquired and occupied by Park Trammell, former Mayor of Lakeland, former State Attorney General, and Governor of Florida, and for many years U.S. Senator. A later owner was James L. Raulerson. Fire struck the home on March 27, 1965. "Greylocks" was vacated after that, the vandals got busy, and finally the City Building Inspector ordered the landmark demolished on September 21, 1967.

[65]

MOVIE MAKING has been undertaken from time to time in the Tampa area. Here is a view of a film being shot at Sulphur Springs in 1917.

WORLD WAR I DRAFTEES muster in Courthouse Square for departure to training camps.

PARADE HONORS DRAFTEES being led to the Union Station to leave for duty. The procession is passing the old Academy of Holy Names.

VICTORY WAS NEAR when this Fourth of July "Liberty Parade" marched down Franklin Street in 1918. Crowds of onlookers saw the military units and cheered the soldiers, knowing that World War I would soon be over.

OLD LEE TERMINAL seen from the railroad bridge as it looked on a busy day in October, 1919. Schooners were unloading lumber.

[68]

TAMPA'S DISASTROUS WATERFRONT FIRE occurred in 1919. While the Tampa Fire Department
was fairly well equipped by this time, it was unable to contain the spectacular holocaust.

AIRPLANES STILL WERE ODDITIES in 1919 when this machine was photographed circling Tampa's City Hall. City Hall was built in 1915 and still is being used. The clock in the tower is nicknamed "Hortense."

BILLY SUNDAY visits orange grove in Tampa during his 1919 crusade. The evangelist is in the center. Behind his left shoulder stands W. G. Brorein, president of Peninsular Telephone Company (now General Telephone Company). Other friends and supporters of the revival are in the old picture.

[70]

EVANGELIST BILLY SUNDAY brought his religious crusade to Tampa in April, 1919. This portrait of the ex-baseball pitcher turned preacher was made by the noted Tampa photographer Carl Blakeslee. The headquarters and tabernacle for the Billy Sunday Revival were located in the area just south of the Lafayette Street (now John F. Kennedy Boulevard) bridge.

MEMORIAL HIGHWAY cypress swamp. Much of the west side of the county was undeveloped until after World War II.

FISHING IN A LAKE in the Tampa area is the subject of this placid scene, photographed in 1919.

CROSS-COUNTRY TRAVEL in 1919 wasn't too comfortable; passengers nevertheless filled the White bus that transported commuters between Tampa and Clearwater. This was the city's first bus service. The vehicle is shown in front of the Post Office.

A SWINGING PLACE in its day was the old Imperial Theatre and Cafe on 15th Street just south of Seventh Avenue and the railroad in Ybor City. It was a notorious place "where almost anything could happen—and often did." It was operated by Louis Athanasaw.

VINTAGE OF THIS OLD LOCO-
MOTIVE is not determined, but it's an
interesting reminder of the past.

OPEN-SIDED STREETCAR chugs down
Seventh Avenue in Ybor City. It was
called "Old 700," shown here at 15th
Street.

[75]

THE ITALIAN CLUB building at the southwest corner of 18th Street and Seventh Avenue in Ybor City was a popular meeting place for Tampans of Italian background in 1919.

TAMPA AND TWIGGS STREETS in 1919. The Strand Theatre was one of the city's leading motion picture houses of

OLD-FASHIONED TRACTOR hauled logs from wooded areas near Tampa when this undated (but probably early 1900's) photograph was recorded.

FIRST METHODIST CHURCH, a landmark in downtown Tampa for years, in 1920. The Methodists were the first denomination to establish a church here, organizing in 1846. Stonewall Jackson reportedly contributed $5.00 toward the original church building. This building was torn down in the late 1960's.

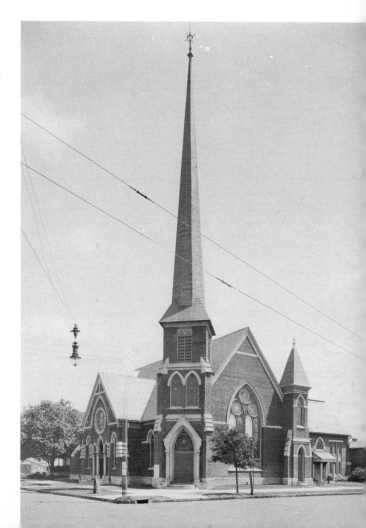

[77]

Right: THE CLEAR, SPARKLING Sulphur Springs Pool on a typical day in 1920. The sign on the far wall admonished the crowds: "Be Quiet, Be Nice or Be Gone."

Tampa since 1920

PIRATE SHIP of Ye Mystic Krewe of Gasparilla sails merrily into Tampa in 1920. The annual Gasparilla celebration salutes buccaneer José Gaspar and is staged in connection with the Florida State Fair. Socialites of the city make up the Krewe who don costumes during the colorful festivities. City Hall can be seen, in the picture above, directly behind the foremast. *Below,* the pirate ship clears the Lafayette Street Bridge. The Tampa Bay Hotel can be seen at left.

THE CALENDAR is turned to November, 1920, in this scene of the Criminal Courtroom of the old Hillsborough County Courthouse at Franklin Street and Lafayette Street. A jury is being sworn in here. Electric fans worked hard to try to keep the room cool and comfortable in the hot summers. A water canister sits on a table near the judge. Noises of streetcars and traffic in downtown Tampa roared through the open windows and often interrupted the court proceedings.

FOR THIRSTY TAMPANS, this 1920 model Coca-Cola truck hauled crates of "cokes" around town for the Tampa Coca-Cola Bottling Company. At right is a smaller model of a delivery truck.

[82]

SIX-MILE CREEK in 1920, where the Plant City and the Parrish roads intersect. The billboard jungle included one advertising "Karl K. Eychaner, Eyesight Specialist" who still lives in the city.

BAY VIEW HOTEL might have been a warehouse, save for a change of plans during construction. Built by pioneer developer Robert Mugge in 1912, the "skyscraper" originally was designed to be a warehouse. But during construction, Mugge decided to turn the building into a hotel. His description of the hostelry on Washington Street, near Franklin Street: "This hotel is a cross between a YMCA and a 10-story bar room." This photo was made in 1921. The hotel is still in operation.

A 9-TON SUNDAY EDITION of the *Tampa Tribune* was the output in 1921. Circulation executives and carriers gather around a truck with part of the load at the *Tribune* plant on Tampa Street

FOR THE LADY TOURISTS, there was the excitement of a highly competitive shuffleboard game in Plant Park.

HORSESHOE MATCHES attracted big crowds of tourists to the recreation center in Plant Park in 1921.

MEMORIAL HIGHWAY was dedicated January 1, 1921. It ran from Howard Avenue in Plant Park to the Pinellas County line. This is a portion of the road from Howard to where State Road 60 turns toward Tampa International Airport. It honors the memory of Tampans who died in World War I, including the twenty-three victims who went down with the Coast Guard Cutter U.S.S. *Tampa* in the English Channel on September 26, 1918. The new 15-foot-wide highway covered fifteen and one-half miles and cost $870,000. The Rotary Club of Tampa beautified the boulevard but the trees eventually had to be removed because they proved to be safety hazards in modern-day traffic.

TAMPA'S OLDEST HOUSE was the billing given this one at 602 Washington Street in the year 1921.

A MONUMENT TO WAR HEROES stood at Howard Avenue and Memorial Highway. It was erected by the Rotary Club of Tampa in 1921. As the number of cars increased, the monument in the center of the intersection became a traffic hazard and was often damaged in accidents. In the late 1930's, the monument was moved to the American Legion Cemetery entrance alongside the street, just west of Dale Mabry Highway.

[86]

THE HURRICANE OF 1921 was one of Tampa's worst disasters ever. Flood waters from Tampa Bay caused most of the damage. The big blow on October 25 had been preceded by a heavy downpour measuring some 6.48 inches in less than 24 hours. The Bayshore Boulevard seawall was heavily damaged, and Hyde Park flooded *(above)*. The popular excursion boat S. S. *Favorite* was washed ashore in Plant Park on November 3 *(below left)* , and streetcar lines were torn up on Bayshore Boulevard *(below right)*.

THE CORRAL, WODISKA cigar factory in 1921 as backdrop to show off two new automobiles for proud Tampans. M. M. Corral and his C-38 Westcott is seen at left, while C. Sierra and his B-48 Westcott is at right. The cigar firm was identified as manufacturers of "the famous Julia Marlowe Cigars."

SIGHTSEEING BUSES filled with tourists pause for a photograph on the Florida Avenue side of the old Hillsborough County Courthouse one day in 1921.

OLD LABOR TEMPLE at 1614 Eighth
Avenue in Ybor City in early 1921.

OLD MUGGE HOMESTEAD at the northeast corner of Marion and Jackson Streets in 1922. Robert Mugge was a pioneer business man who had a flourishing beer and wine distributorship. It was he who built the Bay View Hotel in 1912. City Hall is seen in the background.

BEMAN BECKWITH CO. at the southeast corner of Madison and Marion Streets in 1922 offered new models of Hudson and Essex automobiles (neither of which is manufactured now).

ATLANTIC COAST LINE Railroad freight station and marshalling yards dominated the riverfront in downtown Tampa when this picture was shot from the Stovall Building on Tampa Street, looking west. That's the old Tampa Bay Hotel (now University of Tampa) with its gleaming minarets on the west side of the river in Plant Park. The white building in front of the hotel is the old Tampa Bay Casino, which burned in 1941. At left is the Lafayette Street Bridge with the Parkview Hotel at its western end.

THE PHOSPHATE ELEVATOR of the Atlantic Coast Line Railroad at Port Tampa in 1922 is a landmark of the past. It was shut down in the early 1970's.

THE TOBOGGAN at popular Sulphur Springs Pool offered thrills and fun to Tampans in 1922.

SUNSET BEACH was a successful development in 1922. Part of its success was due to eye-catching publicity shots such as this one of some lovely bathing beauties.

Left: NEW ARRIVALS waiting at curbside of the Tampa Union Station with their valises and suitcases in 1922. The depot was built in 1912 as a joint venture of the Atlantic Coast Line and the Seaboard Airline railroads (now a combined company) at a cost of $100,000. The passenger traffic through the station is now only a fraction of what it used to be when the railroad was the prime means of transportation.

THE OVERLAND was a popular car in 1922. It was sold in Tampa by the Tampa Overland Company in this attractive building at the corner of Franklin Street and Oak Avenue, near the old Public Library.

SACRED HEART COLLEGE was a landmark in downtown Tampa for many years before it was demolished and the school moved elsewhere. It stood next to Sacred Heart Church, also seen in this picture, taken in 1922.

BUSY JOHN F. KENNEDY BOULEVARD today was but a narrow street cluttered by cattle crossing it at Tampania when this picture was taken in 1922. Much of the street side was cypress swamp.

THIS WAS CONSIDERED heavy traffic on beautiful Bayshore Boulevard in 1922. It's bumper-to-bumper at peak hours today. The boulevard was widened during the 1930's as a WPA project to provide jobs for the unemployed.

A FREIGHT TRAIN jumped the track one day in 1922 and crashed into a block of business houses along Lafayette Street (now John F. Kennedy Boulevard). The derailed train jammed into the Thompson Electric Company store in the Lafayette Hotel building.

THERE WAS DIAGONAL PARKING on the south side of Lafayette Street in 1922. The old Hillsborough County Courthouse is on the left. To the right is the City Hall, still standing.

AN ATTRACTIVE TAMPA HOME in 1922. The street marker shows the building located on Comanche Avenue.

IN TOP HAT AND CUTAWAY, Tampa Mayor Charles H. Brown performs a ceremonial duty in 1922. That's the large key to the city in his left hand. The plane belongs to George W. Haldeman, an early aviation pioneer from Lakeland. The pilot figured in the news in 1927 during the craze to fly the Atlantic Ocean. He was the first pilot to carry a woman passenger–Ruth Elder–across the ocean. They landed short of their Paris destination somewhere in Ireland. Brown, who came to Tampa in 1907, was a prominent railroad builder, banker, and real estate man. He was the first mayor under the commission form of government and served three years. He died in 1928.

TAMPA WAS STUNNED on February 22, 1922, when news reached the city of the crash of the Army airship *Roma* at Norfolk, Virginia *(below)*. The lighter-than-air craft was piloted and commanded by Tampa's own Captain Dale Mabry *(right)*, hero of World War I, who was among the 34 killed in the disaster. Dale Mabry Highway, built during World War II, connecting Tampa's two airbases, McDill and Drew Fields, is named in his honor.

THE TAMPA DAILY TIMES

HOME Edition

It First Times

IRST YEAR—No. 9.   FULL DAY AND NIGHT REPORT OF THE ASSOCIATED PRESS   TAMPA, FLORIDA, WEDNESDAY, FEBRUARY 22, 1922.—FOURTEEN PAGES.   PRICE FIVE CENTS.

FICIALS SEEK CAUSE OF AIRSHIP ROMA'S DISASTER

RTY-FOUR BODIES TAKEN FROM WRECKAGE OF HUGE CRAFT

MMANDER DALE MABRY OF TAMPA AMONG IDENTIFIED DEAD

DLE STRIKE ORDERLY

tile Workers Apparently worried.

POLICY RESCRIBED

er in Chief ers Friend-h Police.

N. H., Feb. 22—the Presni—So far as ge, this city, now in s of its textile strike, ng a quiet question. ers and em an endlight hours the upied as they were times. Picture thee uminously good hat-mheen all the cas-ld observe in a tra-sery mill stood out on out of town. bunche of the Merri-mills in idle. The hiahest cotton mill mploying 13,800 peo-teen. Yesterday was he mills, the last la a huge brick fortese mwing 13,000 pen-teen. The workers gath-

The Immortal George

If you had lived long ago and had been introduced to George Washington, you would have shaken the hands of a physical giant.

Washington stood 6 feet 2, athletic build, powerful chest. Reddish brown hair. Blue eyes. Large hands.

In history, this is important. For, without his strong and healthy body Washington could not have stood the hardships he went through as commander-in-chief of the armies that won America its independence.

Born of planter parents considered wealthy in those days, and inheriting a landed estate, Washington was no idler. He fought his way into history by hard work. He was only 16 years old when he headed westward into the wilderness as a surveyor.

George Washington.

He served as surveyor for three years. The pay was small. But George was economical, saving enough from his wages to buy large tracts of land before he was of age.

At maturity, his reputation was established as a thrifty, reliable, hard worker, intensely democratic, of simple tastes, a "square deal" man. The virile pioneers accepted him naturally as their logical leader.

A leading character of critical times, Washington was serious-minded from youth. He knew the bitter hardships of winter in the unexplored wilderness, Indian fighting, and the starvation and cold of Valley

GEORGIA DRY AGENTS WAGE UNEQUAL WAR

Rum Smugglers Are Armed and Quick on Trigger.

ARMED FAST BOATS NEEDED

Dry Agents, Properly Equipped, "Could Stop Traffic."

Washington, Feb. 22—Federal prohibition agents in Georgia are waging an unequal war against the cruisers operating along the coast, according to a report to Commissioner Haynes, according to Prohibition Agent Mack Overbeck of Federal Prohibition Agent at Savannah.

The report describes the condition of the illicit liquor traffic along the Georgia coast and the dangers encountered by prohibition agents in combating the rum smugglers who are declared to be heavily armed and quick on the trigger.

RUMOR SAYS ROMA'S GAS BAG ROTTEN

Report To Be Probed, Although Discredited.

DALE MABRY'S BODY IDENTIFIED

Brother of Tampa Commander Waits All Night.

Washington, Feb. 22.—Appointment of a board of inquiry headed by Major Davenport Johnson, to inquire into the Roma affair, was announced today by the war department. Majors John Jouett and J. McNurney are the other members.

Belief was expressed by the war department that the ban of the semi-rigid dirigible, Roma, destroyed yesterday at the Norfolk army base with a loss of 34 lives, was rotten, will be probed by an army board of inquiry. Both officers and men of the report.

It is reported here, but what we consider reliable information," the report said, "that at least one or more of the gas cells in the Roma's envelope were rotten, carrying down from as 2,500 cases of liquor, are valued at

Dead and Survivors

Washington, Feb. 22.—The air service issued today a list of dead in the Roma disaster, with home addresses, as follows:

Major John G. Thornell, sidney, Iowa; Major Walter W. Vantemeier, 45 American street, Freeport, Ill.; Captain Dale Mabry, 207 Cordy, Tampa, Fla.; Capt. Allen D. McFarland, 729 North Meridian street, Indianapolis; Capt. Frederick A. Beauchnidt, 100 Main street, Derby, Conn.; First Lieut. John H. Hall, Kingsville, Mo.; First Lieut. Wallace C. Boren, Herndon, Miss.; First Lieut. Wm. E. Elfert, 52 East 98th street; New York; First Lieut. Clifford Snaille, 3623 Winchester avenue, Chicago; First Lieut. Wallace C. Cummins, Springfield, Tenn., address of wife, 806 south ive street, Monrovia, Cal.; First Lieut. Ambrose V. Clinton, 205 East Charlton street, Savannah, Ga.; First Lieut. Harold R. Rhode, 421 West avenue, Bridgeport, Conn.; Corporal Irby D. Havron, 3914 South M street, Elwood, Ind.; Private John E. Thompson, Bentonville, N. C.; Private Marion Hill, Newton, N. C.; Private Gus Kinhaeke, 3011 West Kentucky street, Louisville, Ky.; Civilian: Walter W. Stryker, McCook Field; Robert J. Ramsey, McCook Field; William O'Laughlin, McCook Field; Charles N. Schubelarez, McCook Field. Master Sergeant Roger B. McNally, Philadelphia; Master Sergeant James Murcal, New York; Sergeant Wm. J. Ryan, Brooklyn, N. Y.; Staff Sergeant Edward N. Schonnhat, Red Bank, N. J.; Staff Sergeant James M. Holmes, Ashland, Ky.; Corporal C. C. Hoffman, no address; Master Sergeant Gorky, Richmond City, W. Va. Technical Sergeant Lee H. Harris, Langley Field, Va.; Staff Sergeant Louis Hollrard, Langley

ELEVEN ONLY SURVIVE WRECK OF GIANT BLIMP

Eight Injured, Three Practically Unhurt, in Disaster That Left World's Largest Airship a Mass of Debris

TOLL IS GREATEST IN HISTORY OF UNITED STATES' AERONAUTICS

Roma Was Pride of American Air Service Last of Big Semi-Dirigibles; Some of Most Gallant Officers Killed.

Norfolk, Va., Feb. 22.—Completely wrecked by fire and explosion, the Roma, the world's largest semi-rigid airship and the pride of the America air service, had yielded up today the last of the dead of the disaster which overtook her yesterday, while maneuvering over Hampton Roads, and sent her hurtling downward to crash into the network of high power electric wires that wrought her destruction. Recovery of the last body fixed the toll of the disaster—the greatest in the history of American aeronautics—at 34 dead, eight injured and three practically unhurt. Of the dead, 34 had been identified, although many of the bodies of those caught in the interior of the ship when she crashed were burned, blackened and charred almost beyond recognition. These dead included some of the air service's most gallant officers and men, the list containing the names of Major John Thornell, commander of the ship at her christening in Washington last December, and Captain Dale Mabry, commander during yesterday's ill-fated flight.

Shortly after dawn the large detail of air service

GORDON KELLER HOSPITAL served as Tampa's only hospital from the time it was built in 1910 until it was replaced with the new Tampa Municipal Hospital (now Tampa General Hospital) in 1927. The 32-bed, two-story Gordon Keller was located on North Boulevard opposite the Florida State Fair grounds, about where the present Fair's Electrical Exposition Building stands. It originally cost $24,431. The new hospital, financed by a bond sale, cost more than a million dollars. The original institution was named for Gordon Keller, a businessman and philanthropist and one of the city's best-liked men.

THE FLORIDAN HOTEL now stands here at the northeast corner of Florida Avenue and Cass Street, where commercial buildings used to house the Electric Service Company, featuring "balloon" tires of the day, and to the north Glenn Henderson's sporting goods store. The Floridan Hotel was formally opened on January 15, 1927.

[100]

THE TAMPA *Tribune* building on the west side of the 500 block of Tampa Street created traffic confusion with its circulation trucks hauling papers from it in 1923.

THE 500 BLOCK of East Lafayette Street (now John F. Kennedy Boulevard) was to become the site for the new home of the *Tampa Morning Tribune* in the early 1930's. This photo of 1923 shows the old Knights of Pythias Hall (with tower) at left which was built on the site of the homestead of John T. Givens in 1913, at the southeast corner of Lafayette and Morgan. In 1925 the structure became the home of the Greater Tampa Chamber of Commerce and served as its headquarters for many years.

OLD BENTLEY-GRAY BUILDING on the northwest corner of Tampa and Twiggs Streets.

"THE SMILE FOLLOWS THE SPOON" was the catchy slogan of Poinsettia ice cream, manufactured in Tampa by a dairy owned by W. J. Barritt, Sr., which was acquired in 1943 by The Borden Company.

THE *Tampa Daily Times* building on the southwest corner of Franklin Street and Washington Street was dressed up for a parade in 1923. Now part of a structure which houses the Merchants' Association of Tampa, the building is the oldest brick building in the city. The *Times* was founded in 1893, combining two older publications—the old *Tampa Tribune* and the *Tampa Journal*. For many years it was owned and edited by D. B. McKay, three times mayor of Tampa. The *Times* was sold to the *Tampa Tribune* Co. in 1958.

TAMPA AND MIAMI were linked by highway in 1928 when the Tamiami Trail was opened. But many years of planning and pioneering had gone on before. In 1923 a group of adventurers, traveling in dependable Model T Fords, forged the new trail through the Everglades and proved that it was penetrable, after all. They called themselves Trailblazers. One of the great engineering feats of all times was blasting the roadway through the muck and rock.

BIGGEST EVENT OF 1924 was the opening of the Gandy Bridge toll facility between Tampa and St. Petersburg. This picture shows that four cars of that vintage could travel abreast the wide span. An interurban trolley track also was installed on the bridge—but it was never used.

A TWIN SPAN to Gandy Bridge was built by the State Road Department in 1954. The government had bought the toll bridge from Gandy in 1944 and dropped the toll charges.

"THE BRIDGE IS BUILT!" was the short speech the builder of Gandy Bridge—George S. (Dad) Gandy—gave at dedicatory ceremonies in 1924.

FLORIDA'S OLDEST RADIO STATION is WDAE, which was started in 1922 by the *Tampa Daily Times.* The station's second transmitter atop the *Times* Building at Franklin and Washington Streets in 1924 is shown here. The radio station celebrated its 50th anniversary in 1972.

THE FAVORITE was a favorite means of transportation for Tampans going to the Gulf beaches in 1924. She is shown above docked at Pass-a-Grille Beach. The vessel was brought to Tampa Bay in 1906 by a firm headed by F. A. Davis. Later, in 1909, it became one of several steamboats operated by the St. Petersburg Transportation Company of which H. Walter Fuller, another prominent St. Petersburg man, was president. The firm became known as The Favorite Line, which bought the *Pokenoket* steamer *(below)* Transportation Company to replace the *Vandalia* which burned soon after the company was formed in 1909. This photo was made in 1925.

"LET'S GO TO THE FAIR!" has been the far-sounding cry around Tampa every February for many years. Here's how the entrance with its parking lot jammed with T-Model Fords looked in 1922. The South Florida Fair was begun in 1916, although there had been exhibitions of one sort or another since Henry B. Plant built the old Tampa Bay Hotel in 1891. In 1946, the great Tampa exposition became known as the Florida State Fair and Gasparilla Association.

THE COLORFUL GASPARILLA INVA-SION and parade has been an integral part of the State Fair since the beginning. Here, the parade passes in review at the Fair Grounds grandstand. This is the royal float for King Gasparilla XV–D. Collins Gillett–and his Queen, Marian Harvey, who became Mrs. Charles Partrick.

[108]

VAL'S CORNER on the northeast corner of Tampa Street and Lafayette Street was a popular meeting place downtown for many years. This is how it looked from the Knight & Wall Building.

A FLEET OF TANKERS is ready to deliver gasoline to various parts of the city from this Standard Oil Company distribution depot in the middle 1920's.

WHAT DAVIS ISLANDS looked like close up *(above)* and from afar *(below)* before D. P. Davis pumped in more dirt and made an exclusive residential section out of mud flats. The photo below was made in 1924 from a vantage point in the Bay View Hotel, before Davis did his magic trick at the height of the Florida real estate boom a year or so later.

BEFORE ITS SKYSCRAPER ANNEX was added in recent years, this is how the Exchange National Bank looked. Photo was taken in 1925 by a photographer perched on top of the building on the southwest corner of Franklin and Twiggs Streets. The Exchange opened in 1894 and had other quarters prior to this one. The ledge on the southern side of this building was an ideal spot for men to sun themselves and watch the crowds go by.

AN EARLY DAY ARMORED TRUCK used by the Exchange National Bank to transport money and valuables.

THE CITY'S SKYLINE in 1925, looking east across the Lafayette Street Bridge. The town was humming at the time because of the excitement of the Florida real estate boom.

THE "REVENOOERS" win a round in the battle against moonshiners during the Prohibition Era. Hillsborough County sheriff's deputies pose triumphantly at the county jail with distillery equipment seized in a raid on an illicit still at Riverview.

CASS STREET NOW is completely different from the way it appeared in July, 1925 *(above)* looking west from Tampa Street. The houses have been replaced by commercial buildings, and a year or two later the Cass and Tampa Streets corner boasted Tampa Electric Company office on left and the Cass Street Arcade (now Ross Building) on the right *(below)*.

A FAMOUS VISITOR to Tampa in 1925 was the world heavyweight boxing champion, Gene Tunney. He's the tall fellow on left dwarfing Tampa Mayor Perry G. Wall who was officially greeting him on steps of City Hall.

Right: THE TRIBUNE BUILDING when it was located on Tampa Street. The *Tribune* at one time was owned by Colonel Wallace F. Stovall, who also was responsible for many of the downtown skyscrapers.

[114]

FURNITURE CO

Burgert B...
Ta...
'9'

"TAMPA'S FINEST"–the Tampa Police Department poses for this group photograph of 1925 at the old police station on the northwest corner of Jackson Street and Florida Avenue, behind the present City Hall.

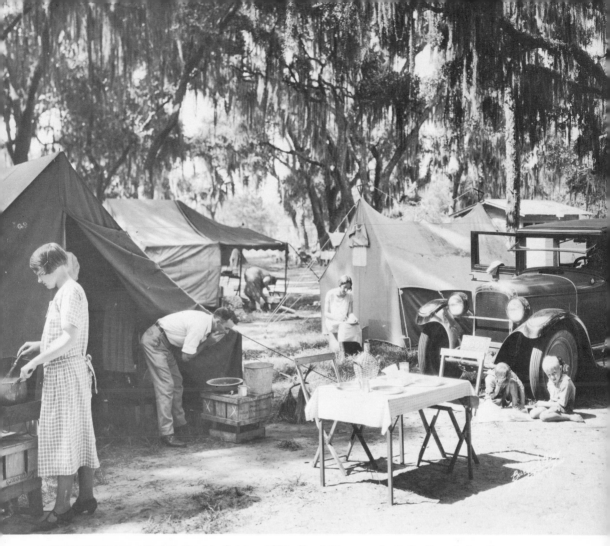

A TOURIST CAMP at Six Mile Creek in October, 1925 offered this scene of activity. It was before the day of the fancy mobile homes and travel trailers, but the "tin can tourists," as they were often called, genuinely enjoyed their primitive outdoors living.

TAMPANS WENT TO CLEARWATER BEACH for refreshing recreation in 1925 *(above)*. The pavilion was popular as this view proves, yet some of us preferred Pass-a-Grille Beach near St. Petersburg as the site for an outing in the summer *(below)*.

DAVIS ISLANDS under construction in 1925 *(above)*. An important project of the time is shown in foreground where Platt Street Bridge is being built. The photo below shows Davis Boulevard in 1926. The island began to take shape by time the photo on the following pages was made in 1929. Originally barren, trees and shrubbery began to grow. The new Tampa Municipal Hospital (now Tampa General) was already built and caring for patients.

DAVIS ISLAND COLISEUM *(above)*, was a landmark and scene of many gala events. The ballroom *(below)*, hosted dances, roller skating, exhibitions, and entertainment of all kinds.

FRANKLIN STREET SCENE on a typical day in October, 1925. "Oh, Lady, Lady" was playing at the Rialto Theater, according to an advertising card on front of the Michigan Avenue (now Columbus Drive) streetcar. Barefoot lad standing on street is wearing knee britches, the style of the day.

NEBRASKA AVENUE in 1926, looking northward from Forest Avenue.

THE LEIMAN RESIDENCE in fashionable Golf View was photographed in 1927 as an example of one of Tampa's handsome homes.

Right: CONFEDERATE MONUMENT on old Courthouse Square at Franklin Street and Lafayette Street (now John F. Kennedy Boulevard) seems to be guarding Tampa's City Hall in this perfectly composed photograph. The monument was moved to the new site of the Courthouse when it was built in the 1950s.

[124]

BEAUTIFIED BY
GARDEN·GATE·CIRCLE

APPROACH TO LAFAYETTE STREET BRIDGE in the 1930s showed J. A. Smith, Inc., liquor distributors; R. S. Evans Used Car Headquarters; the Lafayette Hotel on the left, and the Atlantic Coast Line Railroad freight depot on the right.

Right: TAMPA AND POLK STREETS in 1926, looking south from Polk.

CAMERA LENS SCANS TAMPA northeastward from a vantage point of the old Tampa Electric Company power plant on Hillsborough River in 1927. Boats in foreground are docked at Collier Terminal which advertised freight and passenger service.

TAMPA ELECTRIC COMPANY'S main office at Tampa and Cass Streets had been expanded in the late 1920's and a new electric sign added.

[128]

THOMAS JEFFERSON HOTEL at the southeast corner of Franklin and Washington Streets, originally was the Olive Hotel, before the multi-story annex was added. The hotel served patrons for many years but the landmark was demolished in 1969.

TAMPA HEIGHTS in 1926 was a very quiet street with a few business establishments. This scene at Ross and Central Avenue represents the area well.

FOLKS ON THE WEST SIDE of the city also had a cool pool in 1926. It was the popular Palma Ceia

MEANWHILE, ON THE NORTHEAST corner of the city, the Temple Terrace swimming pool packed 'em in. It was the site of many swimming and high-diving competitions.

Pool just off Bayshore Boulevard, long since filled in.

YOUNG PEOPLE OF 1926 took their portable Victrola and favorite records to the beach for a day of fun and relaxation. This happy scene was at Bellair Beach.

AIR MAIL WAS INAUGURATED for Tampa on April 1, 1926 and an airport ceremony brought out the city's dignitaries. The Postmistress was Mrs. Elizabeth Dortch Barnard whose salary was $6,000 a year. It was reported that Mrs. Barnard "is the only woman in the United States or any part of the world to be paid so large a salary, or to have charge of such a large post office." She was a state and national officer in the Business & Professional Woman's Association and held high office in the National Postmasters Association. The air mail pilot's coveralls were labeled "Florida Airways." Next to the pilot on the right in the photo is Samuel G. Harrison, Superintendent of Mails. At extreme right is Tampa Mayor Perry G. Wall.

MODERN BUS STATION welcomed visitors to Tampa in 1926. It was built by Florida Motor Lines.

[132]

UNLOADING A SPORTY NEW FORD at the Kreiss Terminal in Tampa was this freighter in 1926. A number of chassis are seen already unloaded onto the docks.

JACK DEMPSEY TRAINS IN TAMPA in 1926. A stunt to publicize the new Forest Hills real estate development featured a "complimentary boxing exhibition" between Champion Jack Dempsey and a sparring mate. Thousands were on hand to witness the exciting event. The promoter of this high-class residential community was B. L. Hamner.

"MILLION DOLLAR BAND" is what they called the concert band of director Colonel Harold B. Bachman. These fine musicians played in Plant Park during the winter seasons in the mid-1920's under contract to the Tampa Board of Trade. As many as 5,000 persons would jam the park on Sundays for the concerts. The band was on the road all over the United States with a Chautauqua unit during the summer, and publicized Tampa along the way. Bachman later became director of the University of Florida Band.

OTHER ATTRACTIONS pulled crowds to Plant Park, including the annual Easter Sunrise Service sponsored by the Egypt Temple Shrine.

Following page: TRAFFIC JAMS did occur in the "good old days" on Lafayette Street on holidays in the 1920's when automobiles and streetcars backed up while the drawbridge over the Hillsborough River was raised.

Burgert Bros
Tampa

HILLSBOROUGH HIGH SCHOOL *(above)*, a million dollar structure of which all Hillsborough County was proud, was built in 1928. The handsome red brick building still serves the school on the north end of the city. PLANT HIGH SCHOOL *(below)*, was opened on the west side in 1928 and the campus was bustling when this picture was made in 1933. The school was named in honor of Henry B. Plant.

SULPHUR SPRINGS business district hasn't changed much from the time this picture was taken in the 1930s. The Sulphur Springs Arcade Building on the left still stands.

WILLIAMS CORNER, a well-stocked newsstand, on the southeast corner of Florida Ave. and Zack Street in 1929.

[139]

Inspiration Pictures, Inc. *presents* HENRY KING'S "HELL HARBOR"
with LUPE VELEZ, JEAN HERSHOLT, JOHN HOLLAND

"HELL'S HARBOR" was the name of a movie filmed at Tampa's Rocky Point in 1929 *(above right)*, starring the Spanish bombshell, Lupe Velez *(bottom right)*. Burgert Bros. made the publicity pictures for it *(above)*. The name of Lupe Velez' male costar is not remembered, but Hollywood star Gary Cooper visited Lupe during the shooting. Jean Hersholt and John Holland also played in the movie directed by Henry King. The daily footage shot was developed rapidly and shown to cast and crew in the evening at the Tampa Theater after the regular shows.

[140]

BEAUTIFUL BAYSHORE BOULEVARD in 1929, looking east from about South Orleans Street.

STOVALL OFFICE BUILDING at southwest corner of Tampa and Madison Streets presented this sight in 1930.

TAMPA MUNICIPAL HOSPITAL (now Tampa General) on Davis Islands wasn't nearly as large in 1932 as it is now.

TEMPLE TERRACE GOLF CLUB was a popular place during the Florida real estate boom when this delightful residential subdivision was being promoted and sold. *Below:* view of the clubhouse from the carefully landscaped gardens.

IT WAS 1930 and "talkie" movies were the sensation. One of the all-time great films was "Mammy" with Al Jolson, then showing at the downtown Strand Theater. This theater was at the south side of what is now the women's wear department of Maas Bros. Department store. About the same time, Clara Bow, the famous "IT"-Girl, was starring in "Love Among the Millionaires" at the Tampa Theater on Franklin Street. This new theater boasts ever since its opening of being the south's "Most Beautiful Theater," with its air-cooling and the twinkling stars and moving clouds in the ceiling. At the console organ was the famed organist Eddie Ford. To promote Clara Bow's movie, Madame Himes Beauty Parlor set up shop in the theater lobby to advertise the stylish "New Clara Bow Haircut."

[145]

Madam Himes Beauty Parlor

"SNOW PARK" in the small triangle of land surrounded by Lafayette Street (now John F. Kennedy Boulevard), Grand Central Avenue, and Magnolia Street was once described in Robert L. Ripley's "Believe It or Not" newspaper cartoon feature as "the world's smallest public park." It consisted of a roof-covered water fountain, an oasis for pedestrians in an ocean of vehicular traffic. The park remains today, but not the roof.

WHAT'S THE SCORE? Before radio and television brought news of sports events instantly, Tampans got their baseball scores from a big scoreboard in front of the old *Tampa Daily Times* building at Franklin and Washington Streets (now occupied by Merchants Association of Tampa). The play-by-play came into the newspaper on telegraph ticker, and the electric scoreboard demonstrated the action to the excited fans on the streets.

[146]

TAMPA'S OWN "MISS AMERICA" was Miss Margaret Eckdahl *(above)* who achieved the national title in 1930. She was selected "Miss Tampa" and "Miss Florida," and was second runner-up for the "Miss America" title. Subsequently, pageant officials disqualified both the winner and first runner-up, and the Tampan took over the queenly chores. She's shown below arriving by plane for an appearance at the Florida Watermelon Festival at Leesburg that year. Pilot of the private plane was Jerome A. Waterman, an aviation enthusiast and, for many years, president of Maas Bros.

ELI WITT, the highly successful cigar manufacturer and salesman who made Hav-A-Tampa a national by-word, poses proudly beside his new Lincoln automobile in 1930.

TAMPA POLICE DEPARTMENT sported pith helmets in June, 1935.

Tampa Police Department   June 1935

THE TAMPA TRIBUNE was truly proud when it moved to its present fine facility at Lafayette and Morgan Streets in the early 1930's. In 1972 the *Tribune* was planning a new plant alongside the western bank of the Hillsborough River south of the Kennedy bridge and on the site of the old Tampa Electric Company power plant.

"THE HOUSE OF MANY COLORS" was a Tampa landmark for many years. It was the multi-colored home of colorful W. L. Blocks on Bayshore Boulevard. Blocks ran the steamship terminal bearing his name at the foot of Franklin Street. The house of many hues was considered a bit gaudy on the exclusive residential boulevard. A totem pole, exciting statues, and vari-colored lamps in the garden made Blocks' home a conversation piece for all of Tampa in 1937.

[150]

THE RIALTO THEATER on upper Franklin Street near the old Tampa Public Library. During the depression years of the 1930's, the WPA kept show people in work by staging plays here and using unemployed talent for the casts.

TAMPA CIVIC LEADERS of 1930 gather on steps of the old Chamber of Commerce building.